OPEN LETTER
TO
NEWSPAPER
READERS

OPEN LETTER TO NEWSPAPER READERS

by

JOHN TEBBEL

H

A **HEINEMAN** PAPERBACK

Titles In This Series

OPEN LETTER TO A YOUNG MAN (H10)
André Maurois

OPEN LETTER TO SALVADOR DALI (H11)
Salvador Dali

OPEN LETTER TO GOD (H12)
Robert Escarpit

OPEN LETTER TO A WOMAN OF TODAY (H13)
André Soubiran

OPEN LETTER AGAINST A VAST CONSPIRACY (H14)
Jules Romains

OPEN LETTER TO MEN (H15)
Françoise Parturier

OPEN LETTER TO NEWSPAPER READERS (H16)
John Tebbel

OPEN LETTER FROM A TELEVISION VIEWER (H17)
Robert Montgomery

OPEN LETTER TO MOSES AND MOHAMMED (H18)
Joel Carmichael

*Further books in this series
are in preparation by
American, British, French, German,
Italian and Spanish authors.*

FIRST PRINTING 1968
Library of Congress Catalogue Card No. 68-9703
©1968 James H. Heineman, Inc., 60 East 42nd Street,
New York, N. Y. 10017

A FOREWORD

The Open Letter series was conceived and developed as the platform for an international assembly of prominent people and established writers to discuss, dissect and delve into contemporary ideas and mores.

Each Open Letter is addressed to a segment of modern society, but its audience is all of us who do not accept the inevitable; who are seeking and questioning; and who are not afraid of being jolted out of complacence. Each letter is written with irony and charm; with optimism spiked with skepticism; and with humor laced with wit. Each letter is a personal polemic in which the author appeals to the mind rather than to the emotions; and chides with the épée rather than bludgeons with the hammer.

Books by American authors in this series are appearing in translation in Europe and Latin America. Publishers in other countries are adding their own titles to the series, which will appear in translation in the United States. Hence, a consortium of international writers will present, in companion Open Letters, divergent views, but always in keeping with the concept of the Open Letter series.

OPEN LETTER
TO
NEWSPAPER
READERS

Readers in General:

You are, I assume, a critic of newspapers. Few people who read newspapers are uncritical of them except, perhaps, their publishers, and the most perceptive of these gentlemen are not constantly enchanted by what they read. As a class, however, they resist and resent criticism from outside the profession. The most zealous of those who defend newspapers even deny that there is any general dissatisfaction in the populace over the performance of the press, and have nothing but harsh words for anyone who suggests that the Fourth Estate is something less than noble.

Yet it must be evident to anyone who can read and listen that the press, especially in America, is at a low point in public esteem. Not the lowest, certainly. It has been under attack in this country since the first newspaper appeared in Boston, in 1690, and was quickly suppressed after one issue. The reasons given by the authorities (although they were not required to give any, since their control of the press was absolute) are not unfamiliar to contemporary readers: offenses against morality, and against the colony's foreign policy, meaning in this case relations with the Indians.

Matters did not improve when the colonies became a nation, except that the hot passions fanning the Revolution had cooled and public disapproval of the press was not as often expressed by simply overturning the publisher's type cases and dismantling his press. More often than not, the publisher earned his destruction. Newspapers were no better than extremely partisan political organs, with no claim whatever to truthfulness. In the struggle between Federalists and

Jeffersonians, truth was flouted so outrageously that a man like Washington, who hated lying as much as the apocryphal cherry-tree incident implies, left the presidency determined never to read newspapers again, leaving behind him a melancholy trail of canceled subscriptions. It is a tribute to the need for news, as well as Washington's good sense, that he renewed some of them in the cooler atmosphere of Mount Vernon.

The nineteenth century is a long and often violent record of public opposition to the press. From its beginning, in what has often been called the Dark Ages of Journalism, until after the Civil War, editors were frequently horsewhipped, challenged to duels, had their shops sacked by the mob, and were excoriated publicly by readers who objected to what had been printed. When, with the advent of James Gordon Bennett, the press ceased to be the organ of political parties and became instead the organ of individuals, the result was only to provide a more visible focus for distrust and hatred. At the close of the century, the public had passed through a period when publishers like Joseph Pulitzer and William Randolph Hearst (who were merely the loudest among many) had so aroused people over the issues of the Spanish-American War that they were accused in some quarters of starting it. Their papers were regularly removed from public and school libraries, and there were times when Hearst's volatile formula of sex and politics led respectable middle-class people to believe that a Hearst paper in the home was a sign that degeneracy sat leering on the hearth.

The idea of responsibility in the presentation of news is a development of the twentieth century. One says "responsibility," not "objectivity," because the myth of objectivity hampers any serious discussion of the press. There is no such thing as an objective newspaper; it is not humanly possible to make one, and if it were, readers would be the first to object. But as newspapers have passed from the era of personal journalism to a time when they are essentially business institutions, they have become, by contrast with the past, largely unimpassioned. With few exceptions, they are no longer the partisan political organs of powerful owners. If they have a common purpose, it is to print as much news as possible, as accurately as possible, thereby gaining an audience large enough to insure the advertising lineage necessary for survival.

For various highly complicated reasons, newspaper readers in general do not believe this is the purpose of newspapers. Their distrust has grown to such proportions that it is currently fashionable, across a broad spectrum of American life, to attack newspapers. Often the hatred, among ordinarily peaceable citizens, is startling. I believe this hatred is irrational, for the most part, another symptom of the madness of society; and I shall attempt to prove it.

Let me begin by saying that I am not one with those people who think the press is above criticism. In a quarter century of writing about newspapers and the print media, I have stood so often in the position of critic that some publishers will scarcely believe in me as a defender. There are serious ills in the press, obviously. Newspapers are going through a period of transition, along with every other American institution, and their future role is likely to be quite different from what it has been. But the charges which might legitimately be laid against the door of the press are not those one hears from its contemporary critics. Their complaints are rooted in erroneous conceptions of what newspapers do, and even more deeply in the ideological attitudes of the critics themselves.

Who are these critics? They range from the intellectuals, both professional and itinerant, to the man in any street who is likely to fall back in the end upon that dusty piece of folk wisdom: "You can't believe what you read in the papers."

The intellectuals are a curious crew. Once criticism from this quarter was confined largely to the academic community, where "journalism" has always been a filthy word, casting a grimy shadow on the purity of the liberal arts. It is, I suppose, in part a shuddering away from a kind of writing that does not number among its faults the pretentious and often incomprehensible jargon which so distinguishes academic style. Journalism is still an object of university contempt, although the more progressive institutions have given evidence of their willingness to elevate its standards by supporting schools of journalism.

Intellectualism has become so professional today, however, that it has moved off the campus and into the columns of those magazines and newspapers where the coterie critics harangue each other and those of like minds, endlessly. There, in that peculiarly humorless manner employed by zealous possessers of the truth everywhere, from Moscow to Greenwich Village, they assure everyone who wishes to be avant-garde that *The New York Times* is engaged in a conspiracy against the new society, and that the remainder of the press is too vulgar, trivial and

Establishment-oriented to be taken seriously. *The Times*, largest and most obvious target on the horizon, is analyzed solemnly in terms of the modern dialectic, and quite naturally is found wanting. The critiques in these publications are distinguished by an awesome incomprehension of how newspapers actually function; with these critics, office and trade gossip pass for information.

It is amusing to observe that the disdain, even hatred, of the intellectuals, New Left and otherwise, for *The Times* and the press in general is equaled by the zealots of the Right, who are equally certain newspapers are the enemy of mankind. A man standing next to me in a Midwestern academic procession once flabbergasted me by inquiring without a smile, "How is that communist newspaper the New York *Herald Tribune* doing these days?" Since the disappearance of this lamented Republican bellwether, the same question is asked about *The Times*. One Right Wing newsletter assiduously promotes the notion that *The Times* is a large and active communist cell.

Those who support the Vietnam war think it subversive. Those who oppose the war think so too, for different reasons.

I am not especially concerned about the criticism and disbelief at those opposing ends of the political spectrum. Sometimes, particularly in reading the professional intellectuals, it is easy to sympathize with the publishers who get red in the face when they read this precious rhetoric, although if one has no money invested in a newspaper, the sensation more easily aroused is one of slight nausea. But in the end, such criticism is well out of the mainstream of national life, and I believe its influence is grossly exaggerated. Chiefly by those who wish it were otherwise.

More important is the feeling of the ordinary reader that what he is reading is fraudulent, or biased, or deliberately designed to achieve some purpose which the reader considers wrong. That this is so widespread is a serious matter in a democracy, which must depend on the press for its information. Perhaps this is the place to associate newspapers with the word "press," differentiating it from the other sources of news, printed and electronic. Confusion has been furthered by the gross abuse of the phrase "mass media," a sociological term which has replaced the old-fashioned words.

In discussing the ills of the news business, it is quite wrong to lump newspapers with magazines, television, and radio—not to mention books. The other media have their individual problems, and they are not the problems of newspapers. Television should be compelled to answer for its own sins. Too many people try to equate its news function with that of newspapers, when in fact they could scarcely be more different.

The origins of reader disbelief in newspaper news are varied. Sometimes it arises from the reader's personal experience as a participant in a news event, or his observation of one. What he saw or experienced was not what he read in the newspaper—nor was it, he should understand, what it appeared to others involved in the same event. The untrained eye is an utterly unreliable witness, but its possessor believes it infallible. "I know what I saw," he says.

More often, however, disbelief stems from the fact that a newspaper does not report an event (or events in general) according to the reader's preconceived idea of what is going on. "They're not telling us what they know," he says darkly. "It's all propaganda." The celebrated credibility gap in the Johnson Administration has reinforced this idea, but readers are inclined to confuse government and newspapers, and to believe that if the government does not tell the whole truth about what is going on in Vietnam or elsewhere, it must be doing so with the connivance of the papers, when of course the exact opposite is true.

This coincides with the conspiracy theory, which the controversy over the Warren Report has done so much to further. Thanks to the paranoid suspicions of a few, there are millions of people who seriously believe that the nation's newspapers engaged in a conspiracy with the government to withhold information about the assassination of President John F. Kennedy, and later mercilessly persecuted those who (always selflessly, of course) undertook to expose the conspiracy. The utter absurdity of this idea is unfortunately apparent only to those who have some real knowledge of the newspaper business.

There are other millions who think that newspapers make up news. This kind of stereotype is becoming alarmingly common. These readers visualize newspaper offices as places where editors look for ways to stir up excitement and send out reporters to write stories which will satisfy the schemes of the editors. Some suppose that reporters wander about looking for excitement, for something provocative, and if they don't find it, are not at all averse to making something up or magnifying a small incident out of all proportion. It never occurs to these readers that if this were the case, it would hardly be necessary to send out reporters at all. They could sit in the office and weave exotic patterns out of the editors' dreams.

Such beliefs are usually coupled with the notion that newspapers only want to print "bad news," or sex news, or some other kind of news which the reader does not want to read. The more uninformed among the white population think that the newspapers go out and "stir up" the black population to revolt and riot, by giving publicity to their demands. The more uninformed among the black population steadfastly refuse to believe that any white newspaper or newspaperman will tell the truth about whatever it is they happen to be covering. Twenty-five years ago, blacks displayed no enthusiasm for Negro newspapers, either, and some militants still call it an "Uncle Tom" press.

Among all militant groups—black power, white power, student power, whatever—there is a common belief that newspapers do not tell the truth about them, by which they really mean that the papers are not their passionate advocates—or, as the Communists used to say, "If you're not for us, you're against us." This strange hatred is so great that it has been leading these days to a virtual repudiation of militant leaders by militants themselves for the sake of discrediting the press.

"Rap Brown has a following of 5,000 newspapermen," say those who were willing enough to accept Brown as a leader when they thought he could help them.

"He's your man, not ours," say the New Left leaders to the reporters at their Michigan convention, referring to Mark Rudd, the Columbia student revolt leader, who was their man as long as he was actively defying authority but somehow could not get enough votes to be elected to office at the convention.

"Cohn-Bendit, like all other student leaders, has been built up by the press," says the British university girl. "Leaders are invented by people who cannot conceive of a genuinely mass movement." Sound dialectics, no doubt, but astonishing news to reporters and editors who had never heard of Cohn-Bendit, much less invented him, until he appeared on the barricades, held press conferences, and devised carefully staged events to publicize himself, until in a fit of Marxist self-annihilation, he strangled his own public image.

The idea is not a new one. One of its most eloquent believers was Edwin L. Godkin, nineteenth-century editor of *The Nation*, and perhaps the best editorial writer ever to appear on the American scene. In an 1871 editorial publicly flaying Jim Fisk, Godkin observed: "Having once got into the habit of encouraging people to make themselves notorious, we cannot avoid rewarding them by notoriety, and notoriety has become, with the aid of the newspaper press, not simply a source of gratification, but of gain . . . We cannot make Fisk a person of importance, and fill everybody's mind every morning with his doings and sayings, without making Fisk's career an object of secret admiration to thousands, and making thousands in their inmost hearts determine to imitate him. The newspapers ought to remember that, while for some offenders against public decency and security denunciation may be a proper and effective punishment, the only way of reaching others is not to mention them."

A noble concept, this, but completely inconsistent with reality. To have ignored Fisk, as Godkin advocated, would have been to ignore history, which has preserved Fisk's name but not Godkin's, except for a few scholars and students. It did not occur to Godkin that if the populace was filled with admiration for Fisk and desired to emulate him this was a failing of the populace and not the newspapers.

But there is still one more area of disbelief in newspapers. Professional groups tend to believe that the press distorts and oversimplifies because it does not report news in the way the professional himself would like to see it done, which of course would make it barely comprehensible to nonprofessional readers. Specialization on newspapers has alleviated this situation somewhat. Science reporters, education reporters, and judicial reporters who have been given some legal training have become translators, standing between the professional and the lay public; but the lawyers, the doctors, the scientists and the educators will never be any more than partially satisfied. Except when personal publicity is involved, they would far rather talk to themselves and let the public perish in its ignorance. This policy can be disastrous if public money is required, however. When federal budget cuts gravely alarmed scientists and educators at a meeting to prevent deep slashes in government support for research and development, Margaret Mead observed: "Scientists have failed to communicate to the public the excitement of science."

Politicians, naturally, put little faith in newspapers, primarily because they are so accustomed to a world in which nothing means what it says, or else has different meanings for different people. They are variant believers in the conspiracy theory, convinced that some publishers are out to get them, and that unfriendly reporters distort everything they say. They comb the columns of newspapers to find items which support their theory; not surprisingly, they find them. Richard Nixon's ill-advised attack on the press at the end of the 1962 campaign was only a well-publicized instance of a kind common enough at all levels of politics.

Relations between politicians and the press, particularly where high office is concerned, are always a delicate matter. Often there is a conflict between personal and public relations. It would be frivolous to pretend that reporters are not more friendly to some candidates than to others, and that in presidential elections some papers slant their news columns flagrantly to bolster the support the candidate is getting on their editorial pages. On the whole, however, political campaigns are reported in the news columns as fairly as any other news.

When one adds up the areas of disbelief, the total is a light-year away from the confidence of the trusting mother who told little Virginia O'Hanlon that if she saw it in the

Sun it must be so, and therefore it was proper to inquire of the paper if there was really a Santa Claus. In an era which has come to regard Santa Claus as a profitable piece of merchandise, it is hardly surprising relatively few people any longer believe that *anything* they see in a newspaper is so.

Newspapers operate under severe handicaps. Economically, they are in the grip of a cost-price squeeze with no foreseeable end. Unlike magazines, they cannot increase their prices to cover climbing costs. The amount of money a customer will pay every day for a newspaper is not related to what he will pay for a weekly or a monthly magazine, and the growing number of dollar-an-issue magazines, where once *Fortune* stood alone, proves he will pay plenty. Operating within restricted local markets, and against radio and television competition, newspapers encounter definite ceilings in the amount of advertising attainable, and in the possible number of subscribers. For a national magazine, these ceilings are comparatively far higher.

A direct result of these irreversible conditions has been the numerical decline of the big city daily, the trend toward group ownership, and the rapid rise of the suburban daily and weekly. The face of America is changing, and the newspaper is changing with it. Moreover, the assumption of its once pre-eminent spot-news function by television and radio has compelled it to recast itself. This process still has a long way to go.

Inside the editorial offices, however, things have not changed substantially for fifty years. Breaking news is still covered by the dispatch of reporters from the city room by the city desk. The press rooms in city hall, the federal building, the courts and other places where news is made are still occupied by the usual mixture of veterans and young reporters breaking in. Wire services bring in the international and national news, and the larger papers have Washington bureaus and correspondents abroad. The sports department hums along autonomously, as always. More time and attention is spent on the women's pages, and on culture generally; more space is given to science, education, and urban affairs; some sections of the paper decline slowly, others expand.

Personnel is hard to get and keep on most papers: the journalism schools cannot keep up with the demand. Newspapers must compete with higher-paying businesses, especially television and public relations, and a good many managements are anything but enlightened in their industrial policies. Between union pressures on one hand, and on the other, the willingness of some publishers to employ a high school graduate for $50 a week when they would have to pay a college graduate $100, the quality of the American newspaper has diminished along with its quantity. Hundreds of papers make no effort to be anything more than a community bulletin board.

In spite of these and other difficulties, the newspaper contrives to do its job at least passably well. Its sins are mostly those of omission. National and international coverage on most papers is minimal, and the press therefore has a parochial tone. Driven by the necessity to meet rising costs in the only way possible, many papers are so heavily loaded with advertising that the news content is cut to a mere representation of what is happening.

Newspaper style needs to be changed. Stories are still written in the time-honored conventional way, because so many publishers are not yet conscious that the old days of newspapering are gone forever.

These are among the legitimate criticisms that could be made of contemporary American newspapers. They cover problems which are intractable but not without solutions. Certainly the newspaper business is going to change, in the way news is presented and in the manner in which it is transmitted, but it is not going to disappear, by any means. Its function is unique and cannot be replaced by the other media.

Unfortunately, the kind of reader criticism I have been describing in previous pages, which has led to disbelief in newspapers, is not directed toward any of these real problems. It deals with projections of the critic's own psyche, and it does not differentiate among papers from which little can be expected and the leaders. The dozen or so major newspapers presently doing a job not equaled anywhere in the world are lumped in with all the others, or they are criticized on grounds of pure fantasy.

Even informed and intelligent academicians seem not to understand what newspapers are about. Paul H. Weaver, an assistant professor of government at Harvard, states: "Editors and reporters simply do not have the time to sit down every day, think carefully and at length, and finally make a list of the really important things going on whether or not they are expressed by some happening. It is much easier just to look for happenings in predetermined places, write them up, and make an intuitive determination of their relative importance before putting the paper together. In addition to its economy, this focus on daily happenings has the virtue of heightening reader interest by increasing the value people attach to mere newness or currency. These advantages, however, can exist only by virtue of (and are 'purchased' at the price of) ignoring the basic issue of interestingness versus importance. The result is that newspapers are often shortsighted and misleading."

Really? First, Professor Weaver should inform us how to make a list of the really important things on any given day. I guarantee that if he puts ten people on this assignment he will get ten different lists. Importance is an entirely relative matter. Many people think race relations is so overwhelmingly important that newspapers ought to devote most, or even all, of their space to it, but it is unrealistic to suppose that 1,700 daily newspaper editors are going to agree with this proposition. They know, for example, that there are probably more people who believe newspapers devote too much space to race relations, that somehow poverty and riots would not be such overriding issues if they had less publicity.

What Professor Weaver really means is that background, interpretive stories are more important than news stories, and although he thinks such stories are a development of the last ten or fifteen years, they have existed for decades as Sunday feature stories and are now moving into the daily pages, as part of the changing pattern forced on papers by television spot-news coverage and radio's tireless around-the-clock news reports.

No one would argue that interpretive reporting is not increasingly important, but to denigrate the "value people attach to mere newness or currency" is to deprive newspapers of a role they have not yet lost. What is new and current is still what most people expect to find in newspapers, and if they have heard the bare outline of the news on radio or television, they expect to find it confirmed in print, and with details added which the other media do not provide. Further, what is new and current may also be important. There is no "basic issue of interestingness versus importance," as far as I can observe. What is interesting may or may not be important, and vice versa.

When a news editor, or a team of news editors, sits down to decide what a newspaper will print and where it will be displayed, decisions are made on the basis of what these news executives think will interest their readers most. If they are wrong about this often enough, they will no longer be editors. Various conceptions of the news govern these decisions. About major disaster and tragedy there is no question. It is news everywhere. The major difference in emphasis is whether local news is to dominate everything else regardless of what the wires bring in, barring major national and international events. But there are not many editors remaining who follow the historic Denver *Post* dictum that "a dog fight on a Denver street is more important than a war in Europe."

James Reston of *The Times* has suggested that perhaps we need a new definition of news, and it may well be we do, but news continues to consist of what is happening that people want to know about, and what they want to know has changed very little in a hundred years, in spite of how much we would like to believe the contrary. Rising education levels in the population may encourage us to think that readers will demand more of newspapers, and it may happen, but it must not be forgotten that, inexorably, the broader the base of a medium the lower will be its cultural level. We are not getting appreciably closer to the day when all newspapers will be like *The New York Times*.

What is in the newspapers, then, is a distillation of the day's events. Whether it is misleading and shortsighted depends entirely on who is reading the paper. What a Harvard professor thinks in this respect is bound to be different from the opinion of a businessman reading the paper on his way to or from work.

Every reader, in fact, must bring himself to the reading of his newspaper, and his judgment of what he reads is conditioned by the complexities of his personality. It will not do the reporter any good if he is a model of precision and fairness, or if he has covered the story with the greatest accuracy. His thousands of critics—that is, those people who read his story and have some positive reaction to it—will judge it and him by the standards their own prejudices and opinions impose.

Most readers, of course, do not react that much to any more than a few stories. They scan the headlines and read in detail what interests them, and this is likely to be whatever it is that stirs their emotions at the moment. People who could not be moved one way or the other by a civil-rights story ten years ago now have some kind of emotional reaction to every one they read. The editor can be sure that nearly everything in his news columns is going to produce some kind of reaction in someone, but most of what he prints will leave most readers passively indifferent. Some women readers, he can be certain, will not read the news columns at all but concentrate on the advertising.

The reporter who writes the story has tried, in most cases, to assemble the facts and tell in the clearest way he can what has happened. How clearly the story emerges depends on his skill and on the ability of the copyeditor who edits his story. How accurate it is depends not alone on his ability to get the facts, but on the source from which he gets them. Routine crime news, for example, of necessity comes from police reports, which may or may not be accurate. It would be physically impossible to check all the facts in every such story, and unless the story itself is important enough to demand it (in that case, of course, it would no longer be routine) the reporter does not go beyond the police officer's report.

In the case of political stories, a conscientious reporter tries to cross-check what he learns from a single source, and he is careful to attribute statements, within the limitations of convention. That means the President cannot be quoted directly unless he authorizes it, and many news sources cannot be quoted by name if the reporter wants to get any more stories from that source. For a variety of reasons, it is becoming harder than ever to find out what is going on in government at any level. News has always been managed by government, but modern public relations techniques have shown politicians how to do it better.

Reporters and editors may seldom waste much time reflecting on it, but it is a fact that no amount of conscientious care in writing and editing will save a newspaper from those who think it is engaged in falsifying, concealing, or distorting the news, or is involved in a vast Establishment plot to deceive the people. They will not believe that people who have been writing and editing the news for years know more about it than they do. Everyone, unfortunately, has the delusion that he could write as well as virtually anyone he sees in print if he only had the time, and many people have that lingering contempt for the reporter as a low fellow, at best, which is a hangover from the bad old days of newspapering in the nineteenth century. To such people it is impossible to believe that the modern newspaper is the product of coordinated experience and intelligence, by people whose knowledge of the world is far broader than nine-tenths of those who live in it, and certainly more extensive than that of most newspaper readers.

For all their faults, then, and they are many, the nation's newspapers perform an essential function that is little understood and even less appreciated by too many of their readers. It is discouraging to realize that understanding of how news is gathered, written, and transmitted is so slight that some people prefer the fantasy world of the news magazines to newspapers, or the fragmentary world of television and radio to the relative completeness of papers. Slickness and the voice of authority, whether in news magazines or television, are no substitute for substance.

Criticism of the press is essential in a democracy, and certainly newspapers should be critical of themselves. It is often said that we need more professional critics of the press; surely there is a plethora of amateurs. But none of these desirable things is likely to happen, and other approaches must be tried to bridge the gap between press and public. I believe it is important that the gap be closed as far as possible, if we are to make intelligent decisions as voters in the dangerous and difficult years ahead. An alarming number of high schoolers, according to specialized polls, not only have no faith in newspapers but do not believe in freedom of the press and advocate strict controls. These incipiently fascistic sentiments are reflected in adult opinion, too, along with the irrational hostility toward newspapers.

A few years ago the distrust of the British toward their press was so great that it began to be observed not only in the frequency of libel suits, but in the excessive judgments against newspapers imposed by jurists in these suits, as well as the number of cases decided for the plaintiffs. The newspaper industry made an attempt to solve this problem by the creation of a Press Council, an institution already well established in Europe, particularly in Scandinavia. Through a carefully selected impartial jury, although one without any legal powers, the Council hears complaints from the public against newspapers, and from newspapers against institutions or people. An adjudication is made, which newspapers are morally bound to print, and if it is adverse, the assumption is that moral pressure will elevate the standards of the offending paper.

In spite of skepticism at home in the beginning, and some ill-informed criticism in America which still persists, the Press Council has considerably reduced tensions between press and public, and has made newspapers generally more careful about what they print. On the obverse side of the coin, public institutions like county councils and hospitals have been made more responsive to the legitimate rights of the press.

But this system will not work here, most experts agree. America is too large. There is not the close bond between newspapers and their readers which exists in England, and in parts of Europe. Nor has the exertion of moral pressure accomplished much in twentieth-century America, where public morality is widely admired but sparsely practiced.

If informed criticism, enlightened self-criticism, and the idea of the press council do not appear likely to lead press and public toward some kind of understanding or reconciliation, what other pathways are open? Education, that universal panacea for every human ill, seems like a trite enough answer, but at least it offers a possible program.

People should be taught at an early age how to read newspapers. The instructor should be someone who has seen the business of gathering and writing news in operation at first hand—not necessarily a practitioner, but one who has himself been instructed in the subject. He ought to have an equivalent grounding in how radio and television news is handled, and how the stories in news magazines are assembled and written. Armed with this knowledge, he can instruct students, probably beginning at the junior high school level, in how to evaluate news stories, how to extract the real news from any newspaper, and how to interpret what he reads. It could be an illuminating educational experience for students whose ideas of newspapers are derived from old movies on television and their parents' prejudices.

In reading the Washington stories afterward, the enlightened student would know how to look for the source from which the story came. If it was concealed behind the usual ambiguous phrases—"A White House spokesman," "informed sources said" —he would understand why the reporter could not name his source. Knowing where the reporter got his news, he would have some opportunity to evaluate it. Is it a face-saving statement issued by some agency of government to justify an action which has proved to be unpopular? Is it an advance warning of an action to be taken? The reader is getting more help from the reporter these days in this respect. News stories convey a great deal more background information and evaluation than they used to—although one may be sure that someone's vested interests will be touched by such explanations, and there will be accusations of reportorial bias.

In nonpolitical areas, the informed student would be able to distinguish between stories which came from police sources and those spot news events which the reporter witnessed himself. A student riot, for example, represents compound coverage which few readers understand. In covering it, a paper like *The New York Times* will draw from the observations of its reporters on the scene, from versions given by students, administrators and police, from the reports of spectators, and from every other available source. Out of this large, confused mass movement, producing thousands of pieces of information, the men who write and edit the story will produce a comprehensive account of what happened, favoring neither one side nor the other.

The paper's reward for this effort in the Columbia affair, the kind of thing a good newspaper does best, was to be accused of bias, of inaccurate reporting. The students asserted it was biased in favor of the administration because an executive of *The Times* was on the board of trustees. Faculty and administration figures, at least some of them, declared the stories favored the students and did not give a full account of what they had done. Others thought "police brutality" was the big story and that *The Times* underplayed it. There were as many versions of what was wrong with the paper's coverage as there were of the events themselves. "Inaccurate reporting," as always, could be freely translated as "Well, it wasn't what *I* saw," or "That isn't what *I* was told."

In the Columbia riots, as in those elsewhere, the attitude of the New Left toward the press was one of open hostility and derision. That is to be expected, since the press is undeniably an institution of the Establishment, along with government, schools, organized religion, and business, all of which the hard-core revisionists want to bring down or to recast in their own image.

But there is more involved. A free press is always hated by the doctrinaire of every stripe. In countries where the press is strictly controlled by the government, it is hated by those who are out of power, and with reason, because it reflects only one point of view. In America, where the press is relatively free (in spite of efforts by the unions, government, and the bar to make it less so) the press is despised as much by the John Birchers and other denizens of the Rightist jungle as it is by the young book-burners and anti-intellectuals of the New Left. Their own publications, which apparently represent the press as they would like to see it, are as narrow in viewpoint as those of any state-controlled press. The press in America may represent an essentially conservative point of view editorially, but in the news columns every viewpoint appears. The militants have not been heard to complain that they have been ignored. People who think the daily press they read distorts the news should read the Left's underground papers or the publications of the Far Right.

In explosive, emotional situations like student riots, or race riots, or anti-war or anti-poverty demonstrations, no newspaper can escape charges of bias or inaccuracy, no matter what it does. The simple fact is that the people involved with these situations want the news reported *their* way, reflecting *their* opinions, biases, prejudices and passions. If it is not, they look upon the people who wrote, edited, and displayed the stories as their enemy. That is why solemn discussions about the role of the press in urban confrontations is idle, except in the case of television, which is a different matter.

This, I think, is the crux of the problem. If students at the lower levels can be brought to understand that the newspaper is a faithful reflection, a mirror image, of the life around us, and not a propaganda organ in the hands of Establishment capitalists who want to sell us their ideas about the world, a little later on they may also understand that before they accuse a newspaper of bias or distortion they had better examine their own attitudes first. If they have had the further advantage of studying the newspaper press as a whole, they will be able to identify the few papers which do distort and slant the news, and to recognize this kind of perversion wherever it appears.

I hope no one will think I am arguing that bias is to be found only among the readers of newspapers. Everyone, whether he works on a newspaper or reads it, has his own biases and prejudices. The difference is that the reporter, by the very nature of his work and training, is trying to present as fair and accurate a report as possible. The reader is under no obligation to be fair or accurate. He views everything through his own individual approach to life. There is occasional bias in every newspaper, and inaccuracy too (inevitable in handling millions of facts), but it is rarely intentional.

When someone attacks newspapers for this or that failing, it is always instructive to ask the attacker how he would have written and displayed stories about the event in question. Invariably, the reform represents a narrower point of view than the one the newspaper presented. And here again, as so often happens, one sees the concealed contempt in which writers are held. A lawyer, for example, would be affronted if a reporter ventured to tell him how he ought to conduct a lawsuit, but he has no hesitation whatever in instructing reporters about how they should have written their stories. Businessmen pay substantial fees to lawyers for legal advice and would not think of reversing the process, but they see no inconsistency in paying another large fee to a writer to compile a company history and then telling him how to write it.

Educating the young about the communications process may be the only way available to reverse the trend toward reader hostility, but in the realistic view, nothing so sensible is likely to occur. Sensible solutions to problems are not arrived at in this irrational society, unless dictated by circumstances. What is far more likely to happen is a steady erosion of press freedom, permitted by an indifferent, even antagonistic, public until the point is reached where technological developments combine with economic factors to vitiate the newspaper press as we know it now beyond recall, and it may become merely a repository of useful but innocuous information, transmitted electronically into the home.

Already there is evidence that Americans have turned to television for the news. Polls sponsored by the television industry show that more people get their news from the tube than from newspapers, and find it more believable as well. Polls sponsored by the newspaper business show conclusively that this contention is rubbish, and while it is true that in statistics-mad America it is possible to prove anything by means of surveys, which always seem to show what the man who paid for them wants them to show, there is considerable other evidence to indicate that the television people may be right in this case.

If they are, it is no tribute to the intelligence of the viewing public. Television news is collected in the same way as it is for newspapers—that is, reporters go to the scene of news, armed with camera crews and microphones instead of copypaper and pencils. Television also uses the same wire services available to newspapers. Sometimes the correspondent reports from the scene, but in the case of the news shows, an anonymous writer has to put the staff reports and the wire copy together in a cohesive whole, designed to be read on the air, and a "newsman" reads it. As seen on the tube, this is essentially show business. The men who read the news are expected to look and speak in an authoritative way, to be sincere in appearance and manner, and in some cases to be handsome, or at least photogenic, as well. Film supplements the voice of authority.

Obviously, this is easy work for the viewer. Instead of paying a dime for the paper and carrying it home, and then being compelled to turn the pages, selecting from them what he thinks the news may be, and giving at least a minimum of cerebration toward understanding what it means, television does it all for him. He turns the switch, settles back; the news that the network or the local station thinks he should hear is selected for him, film brings him painlessly to the places where news is happening, and by way of a bonus, the more illustrious commentators tell him in fifty words or so what it means. No further effort is required, and without even getting up from his chair, he can be carried right on into fantasyland when the allotted news time is over. Later in the evening he can get it all over again, brought up to date, with three minutes of sports and two minutes of dramatized weather thrown in for good measure.

No wonder Americans prefer television for the news. Why they think what they see is more believable than what they read would require psychiatric analysis.

Anyone who faces with equanimity or indifference the prospect of losing, wholly or in part, what freedom of the press we possess in the United States—and in spite of various restrictions, it is still among the freest—should be compelled to live in a country where it does not exist, or is severely restricted. Even England, with its stultifying legal restraints, is a sharp contrast.

For if people are to be governed at all in a free society, an unfettered press is the agency that stands between government and governed. Both sides recognize this truth, and that is why there has always been a severe conflict in America between press and government. One begins to understand what it would be like to live in a country without newspapers when strikes deprive a city of its papers for a long period of time, as in New York and Detroit. Rumors circulate unchecked. No one knows what is going on in municipal government, and there are always politicians quick to take advantage of the prevailing ignorance.

Yet, after every newspaper strike, there is a loss of circulation as some people get out of the reading habit and turn to television for news. Those who are indifferent to this situation may wake up one day to find themselves living in a country where the press has become an information and not a news medium, as I have suggested. In that case the news will come from television and radio, both of which are licensed and controlled by the government. True, we will be able to see many sports events as they occur—something television does superbly—but the depth newspapers add to this coverage will be gone, unless the networks do more to supply it than they show any indication of doing at present.

Worst of all, however, we would lose that priceless exposure of political activity at home and abroad, day after day, without which it would be impossible to understand what is going on in the world. The interdependency of human affairs has now reached a point of such complexity that people need every available source of information upon which to base their decisions. In America, the press may be an inadequate watchdog over government, but without it, we would indeed be at the mercy of every man who holds public office, a possibility too awful to contemplate.

If we place any value on our liberties, we cannot let it happen here.

Readers of the Editorial Page:

A funny thing has happened to the editorial page on its way to oblivion. Once the personal voice of the newspaper's owner, it has become the impersonal mouthpiece for collective policy formulated by publisher, editorial writers, and news executives. The result has not been salutary, and in a curious way it has contributed to another misunderstanding about the newspaper itself on the part of readers.

The editorial as such came into being during the first part of the nineteenth century (earlier papers were all "editorial," in the sense of publisher speaking to reader), and reached its first peak of effectiveness when James Gordon Bennett was savagely driving the money changers from their Wall Street temples in the pages of the New York *Herald*. The pattern set by Bennett persisted during the remainder of the century.

Editorials were worth reading in those days. There was the cultured iconoclasm of Charles Anderson Dana, who always referred to Hayes as "the fraudulent President," and dismissed General Hancock, when he was running against Garfield, as "a good man, weighing 240 pounds." By contrast, there was Uncle Horace Greeley's free-swinging liberalism in editorials which may have kited off after strange loves but were nevertheless so influential among the farmers of the Midwest as to implant, paradoxically, the illiberal orthodoxy of protectionism among them for generations. Nor could one forget the cold, intellectual vigor of E. L. Godkin, the master, whose editorials in the *Nation* with a circulation never exceeding 30,000, could still influence the entire country. Again by contrast, there was the prolixity of "Marse Henry" Watterson, of the Louisville *Courier-Journal*, whose fulminations against those who impeded the rise of the New South sometimes ran nine columns long.

The century ended in brilliance and cynicism with the editorial fireworks of William Randolph Hearst and Joseph Pulitzer, but later one could point with some pride to the penetrating intelligence of the editorials Frank I. Cobb and later Walter Lippmann wrote for the New York *World* after Pulitzer's death. Then the drought began. With the exception of William Allen White, whose Emporia (Kansas) *Gazette* editorials, emanating from a town of 3,000 population, made him a national figure and influenced national politics, it is difficult to recall the name of a single editorial writer after 1925 whose work could match the giants of the nineteenth century for vigor, style, and influence.

Not that good editorials were no longer being written. Composing in the idiom of another century, there have been dozens of accomplished essayists on the best newspapers, and some of them are still writing today. But they are victims of the anonymity which has overtaken the editorial direction of newspapers. Such fiery entrepreneurs as survived, like Colonel Robert R. McCormick, were not editorial writers themselves, and the thunderings of the Chicago *Tribune* attributed to him by laymen were in reality the work of underlings unknown outside the profession. In the New York *Daily News*, his cousin, Captain Joseph Patterson, offered a unique (if that is the word for it) editorial style but it was the work of an ex-Montana lawyer, Reuben Maury, whom few people outside the business would have been able to identify.

Today not many readers know who owns the newspapers they read, much less who writes the editorials. Some newspapers have virtually given up on the matter. They buy canned editorials supplied by feature services, which celebrate Arbor Day and Girl Scout cookies, and occasionally the editor writes an essay of his own supporting some worthy local cause. Taken as a whole, the tone of editorials across the country is bland and relatively inoffensive—except to the intelligence.

There are notable exceptions. As many as a score of newspapers, perhaps, speak with firm, clear voices on the issues of the day. They attack crime, corruption, and social ills at home, and uphold the tradition of being the watchdog over government. Many of these editorial writers are experts in various fields. They write with authority about their specialties, and with the added advantage of not having any ax to grind except the publisher's.

Readers may find it hard to believe, but on the best newspapers an editorial writer is not required to write something he does not believe simply because the publisher has taken a political position. When Adlai Stevenson was running for President and *The New York Times* management had decided to support General Eisenhower, only two of the paper's ten-man editorial staff agreed with the publisher; none of the others were required to write pro-Eisenhower editorials.

The situation, however, may well be different on a smaller paper, but there the publisher is likely to hire editorial writers who are in agreement with him. In any case, the editorial does not have the power to shake governments and influence elections, as it did in nineteenth-century America. Politicians today welcome the editorial support of newspapers, but their candidacies are not dependent on the support of powerful publishers or editors. In national elections, in fact, the voters appear to be profoundly uninfluenced by editorial opinion, and in a few communities seem to take pride in defeating candidates supported by the local paper. On the other hand, newspaper editorials in some cities have had considerable influence in deciding local elections and rooting out entrenched political regimes.

As the power of the editorials themselves has declined, the influence of the editorial page has risen, coinciding with the rise of the political columnist. In our time, these pundits have taken the place of the nineteenth-century journalistic giants, speaking through syndication to a national audience. They replace the interpretive reporting which most papers are not equipped to provide.

A certain confusion exists in the minds of many readers about the role these columnists play. To those unacquainted with the mechanics of syndication, a particular analyst may seem to be the voice of the newspaper itself, and the rages of some citizens against their local paper can be traced to their intense dislike of a syndicated columnist on the editorial page. Publishers who are aware of this, and want to present a public posture of impartiality, buy the work of columnists who represent the entire political spectrum. These writers may be so numerous in papers able to afford them that they spill over into the opposite editorial page, if there is one. Since the gossip column has declined, political columnists have replaced them in popularity and publishers try to carry the more popular ones.

But judge not a paper by its columnists. The authentic voice of the newspaper is to be found only in the editorials. There the publisher exercises his right to say whatever he believes about the issues of the day, painful though it may be to some of his readers, particularly in one-newspaper cities where there is no choice. A conservative publisher, who believes strongly enough in his own conservatism, may bolster his editorials by running only those columnists whose opinion he shares, but most are not so restrictive and there are those who take pride in printing the work of writers whose ideas they despise.

The political columnists themselves range from egomaniacs who sincerely believe they are influencing national policy, to thoughtful, informed writers who offer more information than opinion. Naturally, the egomaniacs are more popular. Most people do not seriously want information; they desire to have their opinions confirmed by someone of importance.

In any case, political commentary should be read with at least one grain of salt.

The stuff of political column writing is backstairs gossip, conjecture, rumor, inside tips—the kind of unsubstantiated material the news writer would not dare to put in a legitimate news story without hedging it behind so many qualifications that its usefulness would be doubtful. Yet the columns are helpful because something of the real Washington seeps into many of these pieces, and is recognized by the discerning reader.

This is because there are two Washingtons, the one that appears in the public prints and the one that "everybody knows." There is the story of the new editor who traveled to Washington on an inspection tour of his bureau there. The bureau chief gave him a day-long tour, replete with running commentary on personalities and situations "everyone knows." As evening came on and they sat over their drinks in the Press Club bar, the new editor inquired plaintively, "Why don't I ever see any of the stories I've heard today in our paper?"

It is not an easy question to answer. Discounting the quantities of idle rumor and gossip always floating on the capital's turbulent surface, there is a good deal of hardcore fact which never appears in newspapers by silent mutual agreement. Presidents, for example, live in a goldfish bowl so crystal clear that even their sex lives become known to the correspondents who cover their other activities. What some Presidents have done sexually would have scandalized and disillusioned the conservative portion of the electorate, and although a surprisingly large number of people have known about it, the knowledge has remained free-floating rumor.

On a lower level, it is an irony that while so much to-do has been made over the discovery of homosexuals among minor figures in the government, those in high places have been consistently protected by the press—the same press which is so often accused of rooting out scandal for the sake of a headline.

Similarly, Washington correspondents are privy to a great deal of private conversation which would throw a somewhat different light on admired public figures, at least in the eyes of some voters, but these conversations are translated, if they are repeated at all, into the familiar, innocuous prose which characterizes so much political reporting. Some of President Truman's saltiest offstage comments about President Eisenhower, for example, never found their way into print, but were savored for years by reporters and others who knew about the incidents.

Television has done much to remove politicians from the category of cardboard figures, often to their ultimate destruction, but in newspapers they have acquired a certain gray coloration because the whole story about them is not told. Usually it is not told quite simply for reasons of good taste. Why parade the facts about a President's sex life in the public prints? Is it anybody's business, really? Again, if a Senator or a Cabinet officer is known to be homosexual it can hardly be presumed that he would be subject to blackmail, which is always the reason advanced for firing some clerk in the State Department who may have seen a few documents stamped "Secret" by the bureaucracy.

There is less reason, I believe, for not portraying public figures as they really are in public life, except that the reporter who did the job honestly would, in most cases, be shutting off a valuable news source. Politicians, including those in the highest places, are as human as the rest of us, and they resent being portrayed that way, just as we ourselves would resent it if a reporter with a penetrating eye and a good ear presented us as we really were, for the edification of a half million readers or so.

Nevertheless, something would be lost in the depiction of the Washington scene if at least a part of the "other Washington" did not seep into the work of the political columnists. In the effort to appear more knowledgeable than their competitors, however, columnists may distort rumor into fact, and what is worse, exalt their own speculations to the status of pure revelation. Unfortunately, too, some of them become committed to a particular division of the government or the military, and thus in time assume the status of unofficial spokesman for that unit, defending it from attack, sending up trial balloons for something it may be planning to do, and carefully interring its mistakes, not infrequently by adroitly switching the blame to some rival agency.

It happens, too, that columnists become crusaders for a particular governmental cause, and whatever facts they learn are compelled to serve the crusade. This kind of thing is easily discerned even by unsophisticated readers and is not a clear and present danger to their understanding.

The best of the political commentators deserve reading, however, because they provide the background information and the informed comment which the structure of the news story does not offer at present. They are the interpreters of the complicated, the forecasters of things to come. But they are not the newspaper; they are only visiting firemen.

Modern publishers have found the editorial page useful for another purpose. It is a good place to put the local commentator, instead of in the news columns where he might be overlooked. There are several of these native columnists with large and enthusiastic followings, and whether they appear on the editorial page or elsewhere, they are circulation builders. Invariably they are local boosters, which accounts for part of their appeal, and they are local name-droppers, which takes care of the remainder. They are also good storytellers, and some are genuinely funny. On a few papers, they account for a significant part of the circulation figure, although there may be none who occupy the towering position once held by Walter Winchell, who was believed by experts to account for at least half of the New York *Daily Mirror's* circulation.

The editorial page is also used these days for analytical articles about local affairs, stories which gain more impact by this placement. Papers using the background articles distributed by the wire services find it convenient to use them on this page, too, in proximity to other commentary.

These "think pages," as they are sometimes called in the rude vernacular, may not be full of intellectual riches on a day-to-day basis, and on occasion may be monumentally dull, but they are a valuable service to the reader, and one he will not find on television. The attempt to explain, interpret, and analyze the news, inadequate though it often is in newspapers, is light-years ahead of what is done on television, where such interpretation is confined largely to conclaves of correspondents gathered to interpret a presidential speech or a news event of national importance. Exposing a public figure to questions on a panel show is not the same thing, even though the networks may think so. These shows have their uses, but they do not replace or even equal the kind of informed analysis given to us by the best of the newspaper commentators.

It may be added that readers also like to find their own commentary on the editorial page in the "Letters to the Editor" column, always one of the most popular features in a newspaper, for obvious reasons. There are papers which have been known to write their own letters to themselves, in an effort to provoke controversy and enliven the department, but that is never necessary when the paper is lively enough, or when the news is so emotionally charged, as it is now, that the letters column provides a needed outlet for otherwise frustrated people. Naturally the newspaper's editor chooses those letters, among the many he receives, which he considers the most topical and provocative.

I always read the letters column first when I arrive in a strange town and pick up the local paper. It is more revealing of the paper itself than anything else in its columns, and discloses something of the character of the people in the community. When he reads the contents of his mailbag, the editor is looking directly into the mirror on the wall. It will tell him true whether he is fairest of them all.

Readers of the Comics:

What ever happened to the comics?
Older readers may well ask. They recall a time when some comic-strip characters were national figures, as real to some people as though they existed in fact. Barney Google, Happy Hooligan, Mutt and Jeff, the Katzenjammer Kids, Winnie Winkle the Breadwinner, Jiggs and Maggie, Little Nemo . . . where are you now? Alive and well, some of them, but living in greatly altered circumstances in most cases. In others, dead and enshrined.

Departure and change in the comics are linked to the domination of television and the shifting nature of American humor.

Only the basic elements remain the same—fantasy, storytelling, and the absurdity of life. As readers, we respond to these elements as before, but in a changed way. Television is the ever-running comic strip, the consumer of time, the departure into fantasy, the absurd view of the world.

It is instructive to remember what we have laughed at in the comics since Hearst, in his New York *Journal*, introduced "The Yellow Kid" and began it all. There stood the Kid, in his yellow triangle of a body, soon to be the symbol of irresponsibility in journalism, and himself irresponsible in the manner of Peck's Bad Boy. America smiled indulgently at the Kid's violation of propriety, smiling meanwhile at its own pompous image reflected in Manifest Destiny.

The flouting of society was also the theme of the Katzenjammers, mischievous boys who were comfortably upsetting other people's lives. As for absurdity, saved by that glorification of common sense which has so long sustained the ego of the common man, there stood Happy Hooligan, perennial patsy but perennial optimist, full of the sententious wisdom which saturates our moralistic folk humor.

To Happy Hooligan were added the early Laurel and Hardy characters of Mutt and Jeff. Sociologists and psychologists have brooded over their mysterious relationship. Was it homosexual? Not overtly so, of course. Comic-page readers would have been aghast at the thought. Nevertheless, the ill-assorted pair appeared to be constantly in each other's company. Girls and even wives appeared in the background, but Mutt and Jeff were in a continuing conspiracy to thwart them, and often to avoid their company. Beyond this, they exemplified Laurel and Hardy's inability to cope with the daily frustrations of the world.

The early comic strips foreshadowed nearly everything to come. "Winnie Winkle" was the forerunner of the soap-opera serial, on the air and in the strips. "Jiggs and Maggie" were pure situation comedy, based on the formula which came to dominate that form in television—that is, the dominant female and the inept male. "Little Nemo in Slumberland," a strip so beautifully drawn that its art survives in exhibition, reminding one vaguely of the Beardsley school, was the precursor in a sense of Charlie Brown, and in a projective way, of Buck Rogers and his successors.

They all reigned gloriously in the twenties and thirties, when no Sunday morning was complete without pages and pages of colored comics strewn across the living-room floor. Parents were urged to buy all the Sunday papers (in those days of competitive abundance) so that none of the funnies would be missed.

But already the scene was changing, and the essence of change was the overtaking of fantasy by reality. America's innocence, ended by the First World War, was not immediately replaced in the twenties—we were still living happily in Cuckooland—yet reality intruded. Captain Patterson's New York *Daily News*, the first successful tabloid, was depicting the sweaty, steamy, semi-illiterate life of the proletariat, and in the pages of this workingman's bible appeared what could be called the first modern comic strips. Of them all—"Little Orphan Annie," "Moon Mullins," "Joe Palooka," "Dick Tracy," and the rest—it is "Annie," still extant, although Harold Gray, her creator, died in the spring of 1968, who reminds us how different the world is now.

Once, her appeal was universal. Her estimated sixty million followers were extraordinarily attached, and in strange ways, to this mythical orphan waif and her dog, who moved from family to family in an endless pilgrimage, confounding villains of every stripe. The underlying philosophy of the strip was propagandistic. Gray was a hardcore Right Winger to whom laissez-faire capitalism was the only enduring system of values. Annie's adoptive "Daddy" Warbucks—the quotation marks were never forgotten—was always in pursuit of vaguely communistic villains who were out to take his money, kill him, or both. "Daddy" frequently delivered little homilies on the virtues of capitalism and the American Way.

As has often been noted, "Daddy's" appearances were episodic, timed to coincide with the need to rescue Annie from peril, or sometimes simply to alert the reader once more to the imminent danger of the Red Menace. "Daddy" was also the vehicle to introduce some fantasy into the strip, through his mysterious companions, a turbaned Oriental giant, Punjab, and a sinister-looking little supergangster known as The Asp, whose devotion to "Daddy" was intended to compensate fully for his otherwise criminal tendencies.

The hold these characters exerted over the imaginations of readers was all but incredible. When "Daddy," after many previous false alarms, was presumed dead at last, many newspapers which printed the strip, and even the syndicate itself, were deluged with letters and telegrams. A veterans' organization sent an impressive floral wreath, with a banner reading: "To 'Daddy' Warbucks, Great American."

This outpouring of grief for an imaginary person in a comic strip is eloquent testimony to that basic inability to distinguish between illusion and reality which may be at the core of America's troubles. But it demonstrated, too, that the storytelling quality in comic strips, reinforced by the serials of every variety on radio, was taking over.

The conversion is nearly complete today. Radio and television soap opera is mirrored in "Mary Worth" and its many imitators. "Winnie Winkle" has become perhaps the longest-running serial in newspapers. Dick Tracy, having exhausted the gangster genre, is involved in science fiction, but the basic formula remains the same. Little Orphan Annie herself is still almost unchanged—unchanged, indeed, since her prototype first appeared in the family novels of the 1840s.

The propaganda strip has multiplied, but it is far more sophisticated than "Daddy's" homely defenses of wealth and privilege. Now a strip like "Steve Canyon" is regarded as Air Force propaganda, and its Navy counterpart is "Buz Sawyer." These strips tell adventure stories, but by and large they are based on war, and particularly in "Steve Canyon" are given to patriotic sermonizing.

Mostly, however, the comics are essentially not comic any more, as so many observers have noted. Some papers carry fewer of them than before, but others have more, especially in the cities where competition has dwindled. At the moment, I am looking at a paper, the Washington *Star*, published in one of the only two cities in the United States (New York is the other) where there are still as many as three distinct newspaper ownerships. The *Star* has eighteen comics. Only one of the old crowd, "Mutt and Jeff," remains among them. Seven are serials (an unusually low proportion) and the others are the old-fashioned gag, or situation strip, of varying quality, ranging from the innocuous and juvenile to the kind of sophistication represented by "B.C.," "Pogo," and "The Wizard of Id." To this category, although they are not in the

Star, must be added "Miss Peach" and "Peanuts."

This group represents the next to newest development in comic strips—the offbeat, sophisticated gag, often with a punchline, combined with fantasy. These are the comics' version of contemporary humor, which is satiric and comes in shades from brown to black.

The difference between these strips and the traditional kind shows clearly enough how humor has changed from the twenties and thirties. Here, for example, is a strip called "The Berrys," modeled on the Dagwood Bumstead formula, in itself a pattern for television situation comedies. The adolescent Berry daughter inquires, "Mom, did Daddy sweep you off your feet like Prince Charming?" Mrs. Berry stops her cleaning of the kitchen to answer, "M-m-m-m, no ... I wouldn't say it was exactly like that!" The next frame shows mother and daughter in nubile silhouette, black against white background—another (if mild) indication of the way sex has permeated comic-strip cartooning. In this silhouette, Mrs. Berry continues, "I'd say he was more like any Tom, Dick and Harry!" Then the final frame. Mother and daughter are offstage, and Mr. Berry is lighting his pipe. With a grimace which may indicate satisfaction or pain, and in either case underlines the hostility between the sexes in America, he hears Mrs. Berry conclude: "After he swept me off my feet . . . he stuck the broom in my hand!"

Let Freudians make what they will of this gag line, it would have been perfectly good on television today or yesterday, and before that it would have been equally legitimate on radio right back through the 1930's.

But how different is the humor in "The Wizard of Id," whose setting is a mad medieval court, where life is conducted in a mixture of past and present. The little King, who is the classic frustrated authority figure, complains to his chief knight: "Someone on my staff is leaking information," to which the knight responds with the straight line, "How so, Sire?" Throwing down the newspaper he is reading—its title, in the preceding frame, is disclosed as "Leftist"—the King shouts in a rage: "That underground newspaper knows every dirty move I make!" He goes on, pounding fist in palm, "I'll fix them! Here's my plan." The knight bends down, and in the final frame the King whispers in his ear, "Buzz, buzz, buzz, buzz . . . then we hire secret agent Bodinni . . ." Hastily writing everything down, the knight inquires, "Is that one 'n' or two?"

How far from "Mutt and Jeff" and "Little Orphan Annie," and from all the stereotyped strips of yesterday which linger on. Obviously, the syndicate people and the publishers are playing it safe these days, working both sides of the street. Presumably the old readers like the old strips, or their successors, that they grew up with. Presumably, too, there is a younger and more sophisticated group, brought up on Mort Sahl, Shelley Berman, and contemporary fiction, who want something different—if they read comics at all.

How about the children, for whom this art form was originally intended? Available statistics are not reliable, but it is suggested that they are a minority now among readers of comics. They like the science fiction strips, and those that specialize in violence (not a large number), and they read the newer strips. But what has "Little Orphan Annie" to say to the television and computer generation? Or what, if anything, is the appeal of the other strips of yesterday, for that matter? The two worlds are so far apart that "generation gap" scarcely describes it.

The portent of things to come is contained in the phenomenal popularity of "Pogo" and "Peanuts," in which the new cartooning has reached a peak in America. These two combinations of fantasy and realism perfectly express the essence of what has happened to laughter in our time, and says something about the kind of people we are becoming.

It takes no heavy-handed analysis, with Freudian or sociological apparatus, to discern why these strips are so popular. In "Pogo," the animal characters are anthropomorphized, the first time this has ever been done successfully in comic strips. All that Annie's dog, Sandy, has ever said in some forty years of regular appearances is "Arf!" and Annie's vocabulary is on a similar level. Walt Kelly's animals, however, speak a language of their own, with its roots not only in Okefenokee Swamp but in Lewis Carroll. "Deck the halls with Boston Charlie," begins the favorite Christmas carol of Pogo and his friends, anticipating Beatle John Lennon's word play by several years. The language of the Okefenokee animals is rich and glorious, full of playful twistings and turnings with words, packed with allusions to events past, present, and future. Kelly's satires of contemporary politics, from the Joe McCarthy hearings onward to President Johnson (tactfully ended when he withdrew), are possibly the sharpest and funniest of their kind. And the gentle humanist philosophy of Pogo, who would always rather sit under a tree and eat sandwiches from a lunch basket than contribute any further to the confusion of life, is a reflection of the deep yearnings of many people who wish for the same pleasant respite from strife and irrationality.

"Peanuts" is in a different vein—a strip which has become something of a national passion. Charles Schulz, its creator, is like Kelly in his reliance on humor of allusion, much of it too adult for children; the young do love "Peanuts," but for different reasons. The Schulz humor does not satirize politics and current events; it is concerned primarily with the human condition. The central character, Charlie Brown, is again the familiar frustrated human— man pitted against the unreasonable world, toward which his attitude is one of wry despair. The girls are depicted as aggressive and abrasive. Charlie retreats from them to his characteristic expression, looking out from the pages in disbelief that things are as bad as they can be and usually are. Linus retreats further, to the safety of his "security blanket." Certainly, without being too symbolic about it, this is plainly enough a return to the womb. Schroeder takes refuge in his piano and Beethoven.

With "Peanuts," anthropomorphism reaches its apotheosis in the character of Snoopy the dog. Snoopy does not talk, as in Pogoland, but he is given human thought— a kind of canine Charlie Brown. It is Snoopy's fantasy life, however, which has made him a celebrated figure. As much of the world knows by this time, Snoopy fantasizes himself as a World War I pilot, complete with helmet, goggles, and scarf, engaged in perpetual combat with the "Red Baron," von Richthofen, and his Aerial Circus. Snoopy's re-creation of the clichés of that romantic time (wars become romantic as they recede into history), echoing old movies and old novels, enchants even those whose memories do not extend as far as the Luftwaffe, much less the Circus.

The success of "Peanuts" is extraordinary. Nothing in the history of comic strips approaches it; Little Orphan Annie, in all her glory, was not so arrayed. In the alliance between books and comic strips, which "Pogo" was the first to exploit in large figures, "Peanuts" has surpassed its rival in a series which has run into the millions. The strip was translated into a successful off-Broadway musical, and soon had a London company. There are Charlie Brown sweatshirts, including one in tribute to Beethoven, and a long list of available Charlie Brown accessories. There is much regret, I am sure, that these are only suitable for children; New York adults can retreat to the Charlie Brown restaurant and brood about it.

Snoopy has his own cult, beginning with the Flying Ace gear and continuing in the election year of 1968 with "Snoopy for President" buttons and other insignia, offering the voters for the first time a clear choice whom no one could accuse of being an echo.

By 1968, too, "Peanuts" had begun to appear in the foreign press, which had hitherto carried only the most mediocre of the American comics. Suddenly, however, there was Charlie Brown and friends on the back page of David Astor's London *Observer*, a paper whose disdain for all evidences of American culture is at least the equal of the other British journals.

If the spread and popularity of this new kind of comic signals the transition from past to present, let no one suppose that Charlie Brown is the wave of the future. Readers of the comics should prepare themselves for what is to come. Those in the avant-garde are already aware of Barbarella, the nearly naked heroine of space adventures who sprang full-blown, if that is the word, in Paris and has been seen in this country by courtesy of Grove Press, which has done so much to internationalize sex. Barbarella has already inspired an American counterpart, at least in a sense—Phoebe Zeit-Geist an extremely far-out girl who is somewhat more in tune with the New Thought than poor Barbarella, whose body and sexual exploits are of today, but whose vocabulary is hopelessly bourgeois.

Barbarella has even now been outstripped, so to speak. An Italian comic narrates the adventures of a Lesbian astronaut, a plausible if novel solution to some of the problems of space technology—that is, must the options on long voyages be reduced to abstinence or auto-erotism.

In North Africa, an even longer step has been taken. There a popular strip has as heroine a shapely, casually clothed girl who is accompanied on her international adventures by two handsome and muscular men, one white and one black. It is difficult to say which is more intriguing, the implied *ménage à trois* sex life of this trio or the global shenanigans which are the substance of the strip. For these three are well ahead of events. They are devoted to preventing the subjugation of the African and Asian people by a powerful and sinister Soviet-American coalition which seeks to enslave the non-white world.

What price "Little Orphan Annie"!

It may be consolation of a sort to reflect that the most popular comic strip in France these days—and his fame is spreading, like Charlie Brown's—is a queer little gnomelike character named Asterix, an ancient Gaul, who is devoted to trying to bring some reason into the irrational world of *his* time. He speaks in a kind of Anglicized Latin, which teachers of Latin on the Continent and in England have found a stimulation to their students who otherwise find the excavation of the classics a bore. Asterix has a foil, a taller companion who often saves him from himself—Don Quixote and Sancho Panza, Laurel and Hardy, Mutt and Jeff—but his total effect is to show that man in conflict with the ancient world was in no worse a plight than Charlie Brown.

Clearly, the comic strips, seen in these terms, are more revealing of humanity than the front page. We would be grossly mistaken to dismiss them as the pastimes of children, as they were so long ago.

Readers of the Sports Pages:

This is in the nature of an obituary, for surely there are fewer sights more melancholy to veteran newspaper readers than the decline of the sports pages.

The villain, obviously, is television. Nowhere has the tube robbed the print media more seriously than in the coverage of sports. In the case of major sports, by the time the reader has a printed account available, he has actually seen the game, and since human nature is as it is, he feels himself as qualified to give a report of the contest as the paid expert who witnessed it. In sports, all spectators except some wives are experts.

Since television can hardly cover every sporting event, the sports pages are still useful for reporting the events not seen—local, foreign, or the second-grade contests not worthy of the tube's attention. In the case of professional football, which has replaced baseball in the affections of Americans as a national pastime, the newspaper accounts of the games seen on television seem not only superfluous but strangely unreal—unlike the game the viewer saw, or imagines he saw.

The only major area on the sports pages untouched by television are the columns, and even they, sadly enough, are somewhat eclipsed by immediacy. The good sports columnists have been splendid writers. Unfortunately, their talents only fueled their ambitions, and most of the best ones became cosmic thinkers and syndicated columnists. Many of them, curiously, then became archconservatives or else degenerated further into being dreadful but often highly successful fiction writers, or purveyors of folksy syndicated semi-humorous columns.

It is hard to accept the fact that any real sports fan would prefer the dreary humbug of the sports telecaster to the expertise and above-the-ordinary writing of the good sports columnist, but apparently that is the case.

The sports pages are not about to sink into oblivion, because the omniscient eye of television cannot yet be everywhere at once. Still it is sad to see their present low estate, though it must be said that the comfortable, autonomous world of the sports department has done little to preserve itself. The vocabulary of sportswriting, which once made those pages a dense jungle of clichés, has been pruned and altered to a comparatively fresher style (at least in the best papers), although the familiar vocabulary persists, like a ringing in the ears.

Otherwise, the mixture is much as before. One wonders why the sports department doesn't look out over the confines of the press box and take note of what is happening. The success of a magazine like *Sports Illustrated* indicates, contrary to what some experts thought at the beginning, that the loss of immediacy to television is not necessarily fatal. There are stories to be told which are not reports of who won or lost, just as the interpretive, background pieces in the news columns are beginning to do what television cannot.

Local sports are still served, for the most part, by newspapers and presumably will continue to be, since the cameras are not likely to concern themselves with the hundreds of thousands of minor sports events which, after all, are the solid base under the projecting iceberg of professional sports.

The fan who reads the metropolitan sports pages is not aware of the fierce competition for space which the rise of the pros has created. With expanding football, baseball, basketball, and hockey leagues, to which television has given increasing exposure, the news about them more and more fills the sports-page columns leaving little enough space for college teams, as any sports publicity director can testify. Not to mention the high school players, whose exploits are of natural concern locally. The sports editor, in trying to please everybody, is certain to offend in every direction, and his lot is sometimes not a happy one.

To the editor's problem is added the competition for space in the newspaper generally. Domestic and international news make increasing demands, and with the continuing urban crisis, local news is considerably heavier than it used to be. In planning the paper, consequently, the news executives find that total news space, which is governed by the amount of advertising in a given issue, is inclined to shrink overall, and every day some department has to be short-changed. Sports editors are inclined to believe that they have been slowly pushed toward the bottom of the list and it is true that this has happened on many papers.

The sports department is still a pleasant place to work. The fan who envies the life of the sportswriter has some reason to be envious, although the writer may complain about the traveling, the hotels, the food, the weather, and sometimes even the monotony. Still, the sports department is in most cases its own small kingdom, where the camaraderie of the old days in newspapering has scarcely diminished.

To be immersed in a sport which the writer loves for its own sake is not a bad way to make a living. The world of the professional athlete is a special world, and though the writer cannot really enter it, he comes close. He learns to know well the players on a particular team, and to share their vicissitudes, individually and as a team. While it can never matter as much to him whether the game is won or lost, he can nevertheless be absorbed in it, in a professional way. He may disdain or be cynical about the mystique of sports, but if pressed, he will admit there is something about it. . . .

Sports writers old enough to remember the days of unprotected press boxes, open to wind and weather, and pre-jet travel which made long road trips occasionally hideous, are inclined to be sentimental about those times and to regard the new young writers as a pampered breed, with their heated, enclosed working places, modern communications facilities and instant travel. For both old and young, however, the game is still the same—the drama of the contest on the field or the track, the personalities of the athletes, the endless comparisons between individuals and teams, and the records, constantly broken, always challenged.

There are those who argue that the sports writers of today are not to be compared with the heroes of the past—Westbrook Pegler, in the days before he set out to save the world from its follies; W. O. McGeehan, Grantland Rice, the late Henry McLemore, among other names unknown to the young sports fan today. They were stars in an era of stars, when the twenties produced the glittering champions whose names have become legendary, although most of their exploits have been surpassed. Yet a generation which has produced Red Smith, the late Joe Palmer, and Shirley Povich is hardly without its own luminaries.

The fact is, however, that when one begins to list the great names of the past, a dozen spring to mind. When the roster of the present generation is called, it is hard to remember half that many. So the sports pages slip back toward the twilight which has begun to engulf so many other hallowed American institutions. Countless fans look at them mostly for statistics—the standings, the averages, and the other figures so dear to the hearts of the fan. Meanwhile, the promotors and club owners stretch professional sports to the ultimate limit of the dollar; the minor leagues dry up; the sandlots are decreasingly populated; and the university fields are merely waiting rooms and training grounds for future pros.

Ah there, Dink Stover! And does anyone remember "Granny" Rice?

Readers of the Women's Pages:

The discovery that women were human beings was made by the magazine business, after decades of imagining that they were homebodies uninterested in the world beyond the kitchen, the parlor, and the sewing room.

Cookie-and-pattern magazines, they were called, in the earlier years of the century, as in fact they had been in substance since Louis Antoine Godey celebrated the nineteenth-century female with full-color fashion plates, recipes and advice about the proprieties. It was Edward Bok, reputed to be no admirer of women in general, who revolutionized the women's magazine field in the *Ladies' Home Journal*, with the novel idea that women could think, and what they were thinking was not at all what editors had imagined was occupying their minds. In the long evolution of the women's magazine since Bok, his original approach has been improved upon in a variety of technical ways, but the central idea has not changed. What has happened, however, is a diversification of the approach, necessitated by the diversification of women.

Unless one has studied the early women's magazines, particularly those published before the First World War, it is hard to realize what emancipation has done to rescue women from a stereotyped role in the world. Bok and his successors paid women the compliment of assuming that they were interested in matters outside the home, and that they had opinions worth entertaining, nevertheless it was still maintained that they were home-centered. Women were coming into the business world, and beginning to infiltrate the colleges increasingly, but the magazines paid minimal attention to their interests. By the time Bok retired in 1919 with a characteristic farewell article in *The Saturday Evening Post*, a piece of formidable egocentricity titled, "Where America Fell Short With Me," the revolution in women's life had begun.

A good many magazine editors failed to understand, or to believe, what was occurring, and the list of failed cookie-and-pattern magazines grew year by year as the new *Journal* editorial team, headed by Bruce and Beatrice Gould, expanded the scope of their publication to accommodate the broadening horizons available to women. The last of the old periodicals for home-centered ladies disappeared in the thirties—or at least the original formula was no more. In its place appeared the remarkable diversification which is still going on today, in which it is recognized that there is not one woman's audience, as in the past, but several.

No one believes, for example, that the home-centered woman is obsolete, and there are a number of magazines which cater to her, but even in this category, cookies and patterns have been supplemented by home decoration, child care, fashions, and other interests, and the publishers ring various competitive changes on this theme. Beyond these lies the broad field of women's interests today. There are magazines for career women, for college women, teenagers, subteenagers, high-fashion and low-fashion enthusiasts. Those directed toward the general market once served by Godey and Bok try to combine something of all these by compartmentalizing their publications, and by slanting them toward different age groups. There is a growing alliance between magazines and book publishing, and this has meant a higher quality of writer than ever before in those intended for women.

Perhaps the most significant development, however, has been to add the bedroom to woman's former world of kitchen, parlor, and sewing room. The *Journal* was probably first to recognize that the magazines were neglecting a large area of woman's interests by ignoring her sex life, as had been done for decades. (It was not until this century, one must remember, that it was recognized women had a sex life at all.) Marital advice columns—conservative, it is true—proliferated until even young, unmarried girls were getting advice in the magazine columns, not much of it calculated to improve their lot.

From these it has been a natural step to a magazine like *Cosmopolitan*, the girls' *Playboy*, based frankly on the idea that women are interested in sex and men. The new frankness in *Cosmopolitan* has put pressure on other magazines to recognize a new generation of women, who are going to demand another revolution in the women's magazine business. It is difficult to believe the present crop of college and high school girls is going to be satisfied with the periodicals which pleased their mothers.

Where, one may well ask, does this leave the newspaper, which has understood for some time now that it, too, must reach the women's audience, and in ways that have not been explored before? The newspaper version of the old image of women's magazines was the society page. In small-town papers this is still a highly necessary department, since the communities they represent are more concerned with marriages, births and deaths in their papers than they are with any other local news. The change here has been one of breadth. Where once only the faces of a few white, rich, and exclusive people appeared in the society columns, today there are black faces for the first time, and those of people who have earned some other distinction in life than making money or inheriting it.

In the metropolitan press, struggling against attrition as it is, there is less reason for the continued existence of the society page, and many of these papers have cut it back sharply. The cities are too big, too uncaring. Society has lost most of its glamour, and café society, which took its place for so long, is also becoming a bore. Except for the Sunday array of brides, the society page is going the same way as the gossip column, into eventual oblivion.

Taking its place is the women's pages which, oddly enough, are not unlike the old magazine formulas. Fashion occupies a prominent place, although there is some effort to key it to the real needs of the paper's audience. "Cookies" are represented by greatly expanded coverage of food, but this follows naturally upon the far greater interest in food which has developed during the last quarter century as the result of a tremendous increase in the number and variety of foods available to the housewife. Travel has also been responsible for this remarkable expansion of food coverage, as it has profoundly affected cuisine everywhere in the country.

There are now hundreds of food editors in America, enough of them to have an annual convention, where the food industry woos them with new products. Some papers have superlative food pages, with color photography and enough recipes to make a cookbook over a year's time. There is a sophistication in these pages which would have astonished a woman's-department editor of thirty or forty years ago.

For the rest, newspapers offer mostly syndicated columns on child care, etiquette, health and home decoration. They have not yet ventured into the bedroom, beyond the confines of the old advice-to-the-lovelorn column, whose vocabulary is somewhat different from what it was in the days of Dorothy Dix and Beatrice Fairfax but whose advice is still redolent of the clichés of middle-class morality. One of the charges made against magazines in this century is that they have created an unreal world, and the same thing can be said for newspapers in some respects, particularly in the case of the advice column. No one doubts their popularity, but few readers are sophisticated enough to see through the glib talk, to the colloquial unreality beneath. They are like translations of Doris Day movies into print.

Someday newspapers are going to have to start treating women as news, and then the magazine revolution may be duplicated in the women's pages. It is no exaggeration to say that the situation of women in the United States today, sexually and economically, is a news story of major importance, and one that male news executives have almost entirely overlooked, if they are aware of it. The magazines have not ignored it, and small fortunes have been made in book publishing because of it. Newspapers today devote far more attention to the women's pages than they used to, but for the most part they cannot shake themselves loose from the past. *The New York Times*, as usual, has been far ahead of other newspapers in recognizing the new situation, and in developing features to meet it. *Times* food coverage, for example, is unequaled anywhere, and its food editor, Craig Claiborne, has become a national figure in this field.

The real depths, however, have yet to be explored in any paper where news about women is concerned. There is no reason it should be left to magazines and books, since the best papers have demonstrated that they can do first-class investigative reporting in other fields. Apparently they have not applied their talents to the women's field because so many of them are still editing newspapers for yesterday's audience, or because they are short of qualified staff, or more likely, because too many editors are simply not aware of what is happening.

Events will make them aware in the next decade. It is safe to say that ten years from now present-day readers of the women's pages won't recognize what has happened to the old girls.

Readers of the Culture Pages:

American newspapers have long been far behind the British and Continental papers in their coverage of cultural affairs, and by and large, they have not caught up yet. To their credit, some of them are trying, but in others laziness, ineptness, or inexorable economic facts prevent the press from keeping up with this particular gun in the cannonade of explosions—cultural, population, education, and the rest.

Writers in newspapers on cultural events have always been relentlessly denigrated by the coterie intellectuals who write for the magazines which regard themselves as the keepers of what they are pleased to call critical standards. A more pretentious lot it would be difficult to find. A few years ago when a convocation of critics attempted to reconcile both groups and to discuss common problems and ideas, the coterie intellectuals treated the newspaper people with cold scorn, calling them "journalists" and mere "reviewers," not certified critics.

There is, of course, a difference. The magazine critics use a book, a play, a motion picture or an art show as a platform to proclaim opinions and express ego strivings. The result is entertaining or tiresome, depending on the skill of the writer. It is a legitimate enterprise, moreover, and offers steady employment to people who would otherwise be reduced to holding groups at cocktail parties spellbound or captive. Occasionally there is writing of real distinction, and ideas are exposed which are something more than the critic's cries of outrage against people or institutions that have failed to please him.

The newspaper critic, on the other hand, approaches cultural events as news.

Essentially, he tells us what happened, and overlays on this reporting his own interpretation of what he saw or heard. Daily critics use the Sunday editions to write critical essays which differ from the output of the coterie group chiefly in a less academic vocabulary and an appeal to a broader group of readers—a natural distinction, since the magazines and the newspapers here reach different audiences. In the professional vocabulary, the newspaper critic "reviews" a book, while the coterie critic "appraises" or "discusses" or does something else with it. Whatever he does, the critic inevitably emerges as larger than the book.

In the publishing business, the running argument between publishers and editors of newspaper book pages is about the scant space given to the 30,000 (more or less) book titles published in the United States every year. The editors assert, with truth, that publishers do not advertise in most newspapers, or at least place very little advertising. Here the economics of the two businesses are in conflict. Newspapers exist on advertising, and while space in the news columns is not awarded on the basis of advertising linage from a particular advertiser, or group of them, it is a traditional attitude on the part of many publishers that the book business is getting free advertising in the form of book reviews and doesn't pay for any legitimate linage. This may be anti-intellectualism, but it is a fact of life.

The publishers, on the other hand, complain that most newspapers give little, if any, space to book reviews, and so there is no point in advertising, or sending review copies to papers which are not likely to talk about them. Little is said by the publishers about the fact that so little money is budgeted for advertising in the case of 90 per cent of a publisher's list that trade-magazine announcements and ads in one or more of the book supplements consume the entire budget.

This contretemps is not likely to be resolved unless more newspaper publishers accept the idea that books are news, and of interest to a larger number of readers than they realize, or book publishers change their advertising policies, which have remained virtually unaltered for a century, along with such other antiquated machinery as distribution and accounting systems.

Meanwhile, as usual, the consumer is the loser. Unless he reads *The New York Times Book Review*, *Book Week*, or *Book World*, or happens to live in one of the relatively few cities whose newspapers have book pages, he will have little idea of what is being published, since general magazine reviewing is too scanty and too selective to be of much value. A week's output of books contains more entertainment and information than any other medium is capable of providing, and if newspapers were more aware of their responsibilities, they would be performing a useful service if they devoted a column of space to summarizing (not listing or reviewing) what has been published in a seven-day period—far more useful, one might add, than a listing of local best-sellers, or two or three reviews scattered through the week. Every newspaper with any pretensions to public service ought to have a full page of reviews of the most important books once a week, or even more often.

Reviewing of other media is sporadic, at best. Movies are reviewed in the largest papers, with some attempt at critical evaluation. In the smaller ones, the reviews are often only supplements to the advertising, and it is worth noting that motion-picture exhibitors have been one of the few groups of advertisers to try to influence what a newspaper prints by threatening to withdraw from advertising contracts unless they get favorable attention. Most newspapers of any consequence resist these advertising pressures. On others, the occasion never arises because the reviews are considered a supplementary service. Movie reviewing is taken seriously by buffs and by some people involved in the business, but the public pays little attention to it. It is common for a reviewer to find people lined up for blocks outside a theater exhibiting a movie he has torn asunder and left for dead.

As for other cultural affairs, there are probably fewer city editors who send out general assignment reporters to cover art shows or musical events, but most newspapers simply do not have the staff to cover culture in whatever state it exists in their towns, unless it is a spot news event like the opening of a museum or a theater. The big city papers have critics for every art, of course, and *The New York Times*, with its unequaled resources, has what is probably the largest department devoted to cultural affairs anywhere in the world. *The Times* is one of the few papers anywhere which covers architecture as an art.

While American readers argue over whether drama critics are killing the theater, or why out-of-town book reviews are usually better than the New York reviews, or whether there is any relevance whatever in music and art criticism, or whether critical writing of itself has any real meaning in a newspaper and might better be left to the coterie writers and their little publics, the critics on the other side of the Atlantic, particularly in England, regard all critical writing in American newspapers as hardly worthy of contempt. Theirs is a truly Olympian disdain, of an arrogance scarcely to be believed until one has sampled it often. In England, the leading critics are not found almost entirely in the magazines, as they are here, but in the pages of the quality Sunday newspapers. The London papers give more space to cultural matters generally than their American counterparts, both in New York and elsewhere, and while there are some magazine critics of note, the bulk of the critical burden (as critics regard it) is carried by the newspapers.

Writers, artists, and playwrights who think they are mistreated by American critics should be thankful they are not producing in England. Aside from their usual savage attacks on anything American, the British critics appear to believe that it is a gross violation of the critic's position to take a generally favorable view of anything. The "rave" review, as we know it in America, is a rarity. Moreover, the book critics especially are fond of attacking each other, and the bloodletting by Oxford and Cambridge dons is often far more entertaining than the books being reviewed. That, unfortunately, is the trouble with this kind of criticism. The personality of the critic becomes more important than what is being criticized; his writing is more important in the reader's eyes than what the author or playwright has produced. Publishers, who ordinarily could not care less one way or the other, encourage this kind of thing on the ground that controversy makes readers, and the culture pages are made "lively" by such corrosive displays of the human ego.

In the pages of magazines and in books such an attitude makes far more sense than it does in the pages of newspapers, where readers turn primarily for information. The British press, which has a different approach to its public and vice versa, is much better suited to this kind of cultural coverage, and Britons depend on their Sunday papers, especially, to provide it. But in America, where magazines containing criticism of the arts are in abundant supply, and include every variety of critic from the news magazine mass-market interpreter to the serious academic philosophizer, the critical approach, as such, often seems both inadequate and unnecessary.

While there are no statistics to prove it, granted that statistics really prove anything, it is reasonable to suppose on the basis of empirical observation that newspaper readers would like to have more information about the arts, more news about them, than critical writing. They would like to be told what books are being published, and what they are about, not what somebody thinks about them. They want to know what the art galleries are showing, and something about the music the local orchestra is playing, or the players who are performing it, and not a critic's views about contemporary music, for or against, or his personal dislike of certain conductors.

To this the newspaper publishers will inquire, "How many are 'they'?" Scant coverage of cultural events on a paper is usually justified by the contention that it is covered in proportion to the number of readers presumably interested, and culture is considered to be lowest in reader interest. It is an idea I believe is as antiquated as a good many other newspaper practices, if one judges by library reading, book sales, museum attendance, and other barometers of the culture explosion. Some may argue that the "explosion" is a mild pop by comparison with the expansion of people's other interests, like bowling or boating, to name only two. But it is true to say, I think, that even so there is now a large enough public for cultural news to justify giving newspaper readers a great deal more of it than they are presently getting from most newspapers.

I remember a rainy Sunday in Kansas City when I visited the William Rockhill Nelson Museum and found it filled with people, many of whom were small-town citizens or farmers who had driven dozens of miles in the rain to look upon the museum's treasures, including its magnificent collection of Oriental art. Nelson was a newspaper publisher who perfected, if he did not originate, the idea of the newspaper as a service organ. The slogan of his community-building Kansas City *Star* was "Let's pull Kansas City out of the mud." The museum Nelson left to his fellow citizens was one evidence of how far he had succeeded in pulling the city. Other community-minded publishers might do as much to pull their readers out of the cultural slough of despair offered to them every day.

Readers of the Real Estate Pages:

To make a few more enemies at once let me say that real estate pages in general are a disgrace. Disguised as news, they are nothing more than bald additions to the advertising which accounts for so much of a newspaper's revenue. It is blandly asserted that they are, instead, a service to the reader, informing him of new housing developments and giving him information which will lead to better selection of a place to live.

Nothing could be further from the truth. There is little enough truth in the advertising itself, which is full of outright lies, half truths and utterly misleading statements, couched in the peculiar prose which close followers of such advertising have learned how to discount. But there is even less truth in real estate "news" stories, which only elaborate the advertising and give it the appearance of respectability. Newspapers which take the utmost care in their general news columns to attribute statements made, or to qualify statements they think readers should be warned about, seem to see no inconsistency in repeating the claims of builders and developers without any qualification whatever.

There are few sectors of the reader's life where he is so victimized and pushed around and swindled as he is by the real estate interests. But the real estate pages on Sunday present a bland picture of business as usual, with opportunities to better one's living condition in splendid abundance, and no slight appearance of skepticism or critical appraisal. Only when scandal develops, as it so frequently does, is there any hint that all is not well beneath the surface.

As a consequence of this neglect of the news, which is one of the few instances where newspapers can truthfully be said to be under the influence of advertisers, readers are unable to learn except by experience what the reality behind the advertising is, and often they learn it at the cost of lost savings.

It would be salutary, for example, if newspapers took a serious attitude toward the slums of tomorrow as well as those of today. These future slums clutter the American landscape from one end of the country to another. When the low-cost home builders are finished with their sleazy work —an unlikely event in itself—they will have created the most gigantic potential slum the nation has ever seen, and a great number of mortgage holders unable to pay for it. The results will eventually be in the news columns. In the cities, apartment builders have erected, to be occupied at exorbitant rents, thousands of high-rise apartment buildings which are held together far more by ingenuity than by sound construction. At the moment of their occupancy they are, as the tenants discover, hollow echo chambers of cost-cutting construction whose life expectancy is dubious at best. Scarcely a new apartment building of any size has opened its doors in New York City during the past ten years which has not immediately produced its outraged tenants' committee, demanding that the worst of the construction be patched up. The building managements deal with these complaints while the entrepreneurs are enjoying their profits in Miami or Acapulco.

No crusades appear in the news columns of the newspapers about these gross violations of elementary honesty which occur every day in city and suburb, but the advertising for them, classified and display, produces satisfying revenues daily and Sunday.

The kindest thing to be said about the real estate business in America is that it is a mess, one of the worst in an environment increasingly difficult to live in or with. People—newspaper readers—have been so harassed and beaten down by these powerful forces that they seldom protest even over such patent oppressions as the apartment lease, a unilateral legal document in which the owner is in possession of all the rights. The part that the construction unions have played in the whole ghastly charade is sordid beyond belief, but it seldom appears in print until there is some unavoidable scandal.

The civil-rights movement has given the public an insight into the real estate world, and most of us now know what slumlords are, and we have seen brought out into the open what everyone already knew, that discrimination against every kind of minority group is practiced, subtly or openly, in every kind of housing. (Does anyone remember those distant days when there was controversy and alarm about the revelation in *The Man in the Gray Flannel Suit* that there was discrimination against Jews in the housing situation of Darien, Connecticut?)

Bad as they are, however, even these problems affect fewer people than the millions living in substandard suburban housing, whose plight will be a national scandal twenty-five years from now, or those other millions in the high-rise city apartments whose already decaying buildings will be a major problem to city governments in less time than that.

If these matters are not major news stories of interest to great numbers of people, it is hard to imagine what would be. Yet, unless they affect the current preoccupation with slums and civil rights, they are stories largely ignored by the newspapers. How much of this is due to the possible endangering of lucrative advertising contracts, and how much to the myopia of publishers, it is difficult to say. In either case, it is an area worth getting indignant about, as far as the newspaper reader is concerned. The newspapers could do much to slow down or prevent any further damage if they refused to turn their news columns into adjuncts for the benefit of real estate advertisers and began to report what is really happening in the construction business on a day-to-day basis, not what occurs when one of the sins of the industry happens to catch up to it.

It is not likely that newspapers will do this kind of investigative reporting on their own account. They will if enough readers demand it. This is a case where victims can gain a measure of relief if they insist. If they do not, they will get the kind of housing their apathy deserves.

Believers in Freedom of the Press:

But doesn't everyone believe in freedom of the press? Unfortunately, no. Like so many articles in the Bill of Rights, the First Amendment is given more lip service than actual honoring. Any number of people would like to curtail it, and an alarming number succeed in doing so.

No press can call itself free, for example, when unions have the power to put a paper out of business, and do. How sad it is to see the trade union movement of the thirties, inspired by brutal injustice and shocking industrial conditions, win its battles first for recognition and then for decent standards of wages and hours—win and thrive, then take on slowly all the arrogance of power and its abuses which it struggled against at the beginning. Today there is little to choose between union behavior and the way business was conducted in the unrestrained days of laissez-faire capitalism. Ruthless intransigence is the same, no matter what its source.

Despite their pious protestations and cries of pain that it is really the publishers who are to blame, there is no question that newspaper unions are slowly strangling the metropolitan press in the United States. The leaders of the mechanical unions do not care; there are always jobs elsewhere for their members. The leaders of the Newspaper Guild care, but while they fight for imaginary principles, newspapers close down and their members find jobs in other businesses. The impact these unstable conditions have had on recruiting for the profession has been disastrous.

It is true that the publishers have a share of blame. There is intransigence and arrogance on that side, too, and in some quarters more than a little inability to comprehend their true position. But on the other hand, the publishers are faced with the realities of the cost-price squeeze, which cannot be avoided or solved by present practices. The fact of the matter is that the problems of the newspaper business cannot be resolved, as far as metropolitan papers are concerned, except by a cooperative effort on the part of publishers and unions. The present pattern of strike-or-else can only result in continuing disaster. Union leaders or publishers who cannot grasp this elemental and self-evident fact are enemies of freedom of the press.

Government is another enemy. How can there be real freedom of the press when a petty county official can deny a reporter from a local newspaper access to public records? How can it be free when the bureaucrats of the federal government are permitted to decide by rubber stamp what uses of public money the taxpayers are permitted to learn about, on the spurious plea of "security"? Can it be freedom when the operation of a freely elected government cannot be scrutinized because that government carefully selects the facts about itself that it wants the public to know? Or worse, deliberately lies to the voters through the information media? All these things happen every day in the American government. They are almost a matter of routine. Publishers fight against them, but not hard enough. Forming a Freedom of Information Committee is worthy and useful, but it cannot take the place of a continuing, united, hard-hitting crusade, in the nineteenth-century style, against the abuses of governmental power.

The reasons for failure are both political and personal. Since the press is predominantly conservative and Republican, much of its struggle against government has a political coloration. It is too often a matter of getting at the damned Democrats instead of opening channels of information to the public about the government they are taxed to support. In a personal sense, the publishers too often are on a basis of friendship with governmental leaders, and like the cronyism of old City Hall reporters with the rascals whose movements they are supposed to regard with suspicion, it is hard for the publishers to say something nasty about old Joe even when he has done something stupid or venal. Moreover, the friendliness which develops between Washington reporters and their news sources often stands in the way of the objective view of what these sources are up to. It ought to be the basic premise of political reporting that governments are guilty of impeding the rational functioning of society until proven innocent. In this country government governs by the consent of the governed, but not necessarily for their benefit.

Newspapers themselves are sometimes the enemy of freedom of the press. It is incongruous, for instance, that *The New York Times* should by policy fiat prevent the reviewing or advertising of books about sex education or information in its *Book Review*, while at the same time it welcomes advertising twice as provocative in itself for motion pictures. Inconsistent, obviously, but also a direct violation of the responsibility implied in the First Amendment's guarantee, no matter how it may be rationalized. It is a melancholy truism that publishers cry out against government interference with press freedom, but when they themselves interfere, they retreat to the contention that they are, after all, a private business.

Recently the long-standing enmity of the bench and bar toward the press has erupted in a controversy over the handling of court proceedings. This argument is clothed in elaborate rhetoric about the rights of defendants and the necessity to have unprejudiced juries (a monstrous absurdity in itself), but underneath the polite language of the controversy is the blunt fact that the law, like government, wants to run its own business in its own way without any interference from the press.

In another sense, newspaper readers are enemies of freedom of the press. By their apathy, and their refusal to demand that newspapers fulfill the obligations and responsibilities imposed on them by the First Amendment's protection, they limit the freedom of newspapers. Readers ought to remember that the newspaper is, or should be, their lobby in government, their pleader of causes against the monolithic institutions of society which otherwise are not responsive. Newspapers can be, and still are sometimes, instruments of social justice and social change. They reflect the people they serve, and at the same time are as much of a real voice as the population possesses. If readers understood this reality instead of berating and distrusting the newspapers as merely another of their many enemies, a powerful alliance between press and public could be formed which would be a political weapon of extreme potency.

I have little faith that such a union is going to occur. If it is true that people get the kind of government they deserve, it is equally true that the press is more truly a reflection of themselves than they are willing to believe. We shall see. Occasionally, in the history of the world, events compel the most unlikely reforms.

* * *

In reading over these fragmentary letters, I find that there is something in them calculated to offend everyone. I cannot imagine my book will be overwhelmingly popular with any category of readers. Assuming that they take the trouble to read it. But after twenty-five books or so, and having reached the comfortable age where it is no longer necessary to prove anything, I am not especially concerned with the popularity of either book or author. What I would hope for, most earnestly, is that these letters would arouse some concern about the press on the part of those who read it. For in the end, reader apathy is its chief enemy, and newspapers are far too important a medium in a democracy to be permitted to wither away or change into something innocuous without a struggle.

Newspaper readers, unite! You have nothing to lose but your democratic rights.

What do you think of *Open Letter to Newspaper Readers?* Of the opinions expressed in it? Of John Tebbel's point of view?

Do you find Mr. Tebbel's arguments well-founded or fallacious? Do you feel that *Open Letter to Newspaper Readers* takes its proper place in the Open Letter series whose purpose is to "discuss, dissect and delve into contemporary ideas and mores?"

Give us your opinions on *Open Letter to Newspaper Readers*. We will be more than happy to discuss them with you, and we will invite John Tebbel to write to you, too.

JAMES H. HEINEMAN, INC.
60 East 42nd Street
New York, N.Y. 10017

PN 4867 .T4 1968

PN 4867 .T4 1968

AUTHOR

TITLE Tebbel, John William
Open Letter to
Newspaper Readers